CU00750074

Cop

Gil & Renee M.

For permissions requests or inquiries, please contact Gil & Renee M. Beavers at Help@richrelationshipsrefuge.com

Published by RICH RR LLC.

ISBN: 979-8-218-42521-0

FOREWORD

Welcome to the "Singles Blueprint for Dating and Marriage" brought to you by Rich Relationships Refuge. We are thrilled to embark on this journey with you a journey that encompasses the complexities, joys, and sacredness of seeking and nurturing lasting love.

As marriage mentors and founders of Rich Relationships Refuge, we have had the privilege of walking alongside countless couples as they navigate the beautiful and sometimes challenging path of love. Over the years, we've witnessed firsthand the transformative power of intentional,

Christ centered relationships the kind that not only withstand the tests of time but also blossom into lifelong partnerships filled with joy, fulfillment, and purpose.

But we also understand that the road to love is not always easy. It's fraught with uncertainties, doubts, and obstacles that can sometimes feel insurmountable. That's why we've created the "Singles Blueprint for Dating and Marriage" to provide you with practical guidance, spiritual insights, and real-world illustrations to help you navigate the complexities of dating and prepare for the sacred journey of marriage.

In this blueprint, you'll find a wealth of wisdom gleaned from our own experiences, as well as from the couples we've had the honor of serving over the years. Each chapter is crafted with care and intentionality, addressing key aspects of the dating and relationship journey from initial attraction to building a strong foundation, from overcoming obstacles to embracing God's design for marriage.

But more than just a guidebook, the "Singles Blueprint" is a community a place where you can find encouragement, support, and camaraderie as you embark on this journey of love. We invite you to lean into the wisdom of our mentors, engage with the stories and experiences shared within these pages, and connect with others who are walking the same path.

As you dive into the "Singles Blueprint," we encourage you to approach this journey with an open heart, a teachable spirit, and a commitment to honoring God in all that you do. Remember that you are not alone God is with you every step of the way, guiding, comforting, and empowering you to embrace His best for your life.

So, whether you're single and seeking, dating and discerning, or engaged and preparing for marriage, we hope that the "Singles Blueprint for Dating and Marriage" will be a source of inspiration, encouragement, and empowerment as you pursue God's plan for your love story.

May this blueprint serve as a guiding light on your journey to everlasting love a love that reflects the beauty, grace, and faithfulness of our Savior, Jesus Christ.

With love and blessings,

Gil & Renée M Beavers

Founders, Rich Relationships Refuge

DEDICATION

To our beloved daughter Aharon, our precious niece Lyric, our cherished nephew Elijah, and the vibrant RICH Relationships Refuge Community,

In the tapestry of our lives, each of you holds a unique and cherished place. Aharon, your journey has been one of twists and turns, challenges and triumphs. Through it all, your courage, resilience, and unwavering spirit have shone brightly, inspiring us to never lose hope and to always believe in the power of redemption and renewal.

Lyric and Elijah, your youthful innocence, boundless energy, and endless curiosity bring light and joy into our lives. Your presence reminds us of the beauty and wonder that surrounds us each day, and we are grateful for the love and laughter you bring into our home.

To our RICH Relationships Refuge Community, you are the heart and soul of our shared journey. Your support, understanding, and unwavering presence have been a source of strength and comfort during both the highs and lows of life. Together, we create a space of warmth, acceptance, and growth a sanctuary where love flourishes, and connections deepen.

May the wisdom shared within these pages serve as a guiding light for you all Aharon, Lyric, Elijah, and our RICH Community. May you continue to nurture your relationships with kindness, compassion, and grace, knowing that you are surrounded by a circle of love and support that knows no bounds.

With boundless love and unwavering faith,

Gil & Renée Beavers
RICH Relationships Refuge

Our Relationship
with Change

Renée M. Beavers

I am Renée M. Beavers, a fifty-two-year-old woman, whose hometown is Detroit, Michigan. Gilbert (Gil), my husband, and I are a retired Air Force family who has lived in thirteen cities in the U.S. and overseas. Due to our travels, I had to turn my back from the mundane and what made me comfortable to embrace the unfamiliar to grow. I had to become comfortable with being uncomfortable. I have experienced different cultures, traditions, and people in my lifetime.

I loved growing up in a big city. I have lived in small towns as well. While living in a big city can make you open to new ideas and cultures, I love the closeness I observed in small towns the traditions and lifelong relationships. However, living in a small town can make you closedminded to new people and experiences. There must be a balance between remaining open to change while maintaining a commitment to your core values and healthy relationships. Living our lives with grace for differences makes us kind and ensures we will continue to improve and mature.

I am choosing to give myself permission to live well and overcome vitiligo, celiac disease, and osteoarthritis. Making food my medicine was my bravest moment. Pain, sickness, and an adverse medical condition can get our attention, unlike anything else. I gave up my twenty-eight-year career as a Salon Owner & Hair Care Professional to become an author, speaker, and food evangelist. Living daily with food as a medicine and not a prescription drug was my wisest decision. My commitment to change my life has positioned me to lead others on a journey of learning the power of food as medicine. This choice has taught me that life is a journey, not a destination or an event. We are growing and changing becoming the person God created us to become, one decision, and sometimes, one career at a time.

Being a woman has held me back because I am called into a man's world. Public speaking and evangelism are positions usually held by men. Even getting the help needed from my doctors was affected by my being a woman. Some of my medical professionals overlooked my symptoms. Sometimes women are not taken as seriously as men when they make medical claims.

While these obvious barriers have made things difficult, they have also strengthened me. It has forced me to study harder, gather more evidence-based data, and it has motivated me to create a solution-based program. I love being a woman. I know I am unique and one of a kind!

The greatest strength any woman can possess is the power to know and love the reflection in the mirror from the inside out. The love I have for myself permeates my relationships. My life is full! The two men whose support and love mean the most, have put their seal in my heart and mind. Thank you, Abba God, and Gil, you are my everything. That love empowered me to love, nurture and care for others. I am created for greatness and with that same knowledge, I am empowered, and I empower and lift others up.

If I had to summarize my life in one dream, it would be that my life would make a difference forever and into eternity and that I would not only be successful in relationships but also with God's resources. Becoming an author is a lifelong dream I did not realize I had. As an author, I will accomplish my life dream. Writing books makes you eternal; it has actualized my lifelong dream. My life and all the people and the events of my life will live on forever in my books providing love, hope, freedom, and liberty to its readers.

My Mantra: Live Life with Fewer Regrets

This will come as a shock to people that do not know me and it will be painful for the people who do. Nonetheless, it is my truth. Two selfish people who were addicted to drugs raised me. I had to grow up fast and I was a parent to my young siblings. Not only did I proclaim and profess that I would never have children, I did not even like people who had children. I talk about living a life with fewer regrets. If I had to say what my biggest regret is, it would be that I allowed the death of my beloved Godmother to make me lie to myself about who I was and who I was not. Her belief was every woman should leave their mark on the world by having a child.

I did not share this belief but her death made me act as if I did. The girl who hated her mom, would now become a mother, how sad? No, I do not regret our daughter! I regret why and when we had her. I now know what you do is not as important as when and why you do it. Yes, all things work for good for those who love God. It does not erase the consequences and I must unpack those consequences of each choice I make. I was twenty-one when we got married and twenty-three when we had our daughter. I know now, you can never be too old or too young for a task but you can be too hurt.

My decision to have a child was not from my deep love and adoration for my amazing husband. It was from the deep hurt and loss of my Godmother. She did not give birth to me but she imparted life into my being. I did not know at twenty-three what I know today. Before our daughter would reach ten months old, a serial killer took my mother's life and my stepfather died of cancer. My twenty-three-year-old husband and I faced the decision to adopt my then nine- and ten-year-old sisters. Again, the decision to parent was paired with pain, hurt, and death. Unfortunately, we committed a betrayal against ourselves and adopted two girls.

Yes, they were my flesh and blood but strangers, nonetheless.

I moved away from home when I was eighteen and got married when I was twenty-one.

My husband and I were the people who sent nice gifts for birthdays and Christmas we were not their parents. The decision for when and why to become a parent is my biggest regret. Unfortunately, I would say parenting has and still is my most significant area of growth. Our decisions must be ours. We must choose our why and commit to our why.

Are you happy? Happy means everything is going as planned. By that definition, I have never been or will never be happy. In my life, things do not go as planned. I have allowed joy to fuel and govern my life. I am overwhelmed with joy each day. I am an overachiever; I love processes, order and results. I must remind myself daily that the process of life is the journey, and without the process, I would not have established the stamina to thrive once I reach a destination. In life, there are different destinations for different stages in life.

I married my best friend and learned to be a good listener and practice what I heard. Love is a choice. It makes our life and relationships count.

Building something that did not exist for something you have never seen for people who do not want it is challenging. Having this same assignment take years to grow can become discouraging. This is what the Freedom from Food Program is. I am new to the roles of Author, Speaker, and Teacher, and so is my Relationship Lifestyle Movement. I want to fight for people's healthy relationships, not fight with them about it. My daily challenge is not whether to quit every day, but should I begin each day again?

I spark awareness, encourage taking responsibility, and I empower individuals to make choices that support healthy choices and relationships. I love God and people.

How, Who, Why?

The answer to these three questions can make or break us. Today, I am a Christ follower! I am a wife, mother, sister, friend, entrepreneur, author, and lifestyle strategist. With so many titles as women, we must discover our why. After owning and building salons for twenty-eight years, I have realized that I found my identity not in my God given purpose, but in my ability to generate income. Living your life motivated by "How" and money is exhausting in our information driven societies. There are millions of how to have ideas. Most of them will produce results. Yet, "How" without "Why" is like a day without night! It is out of order and it will wear you out.

WARNING: The information that we are about to share with you will most likely sound unrealistic and even unattainable. However, we strongly urge to read through this information and most importantly apply these principles to your everyday life and watch how you and your relationships change for your good and God's glory!

The How Is Easy

I know who I am! Learning "How" to achieve a task or goal is also somewhat easy to do if we don't take the long journey inward to discover our "Why."

I loved doing hair and I was good at it; and yes, I made a lot of money. If you asked me during that time about my life, I would have shared that I was living "My Best Life." The keyword is I was living 'my' best life! Not for God, but for me and mine only. Being comfortable can be so dangerous. In our comfort, we are not dependent on hearing God or even asking Him for our next step.

I would always brag and say I could do hair with my eyes closed! That is an extremely dangerous place to remain.

We grow when we are stretched, challenged, and uncomfortable. My books, website, social media, group and individual sessions are how we share our results-based solutions. I am driven to learn lessons and lead myself and others into true life change with fewer regrets.

Obstacles strengthen us and they are as valuable as our opportunities. My biggest obstacle in life is failing to get to the root of my obstacles and my pain. God will call each of His children out into the deep, off the sidelines, and yes, to do something that makes us feel uncomfortable. Life is unfair. We will all have horrible tragic things that will happen in our lifetime and they will hurt us. What we do with our hurt differentiates and defines us. Yeah, there is always pain and difficulty knitted into our good news. It makes us sober and grateful.

Our Why

Our "Why" will also have to determine our "How"? "How" will rule our lives and crowd out our intimacy with God, ourselves, and others. Also, it's important to determine who we are.

Today, I am becoming the woman God designed me to become. The things that scared me to death are now a part of my daily life. I write books, speak in front of large and small groups, and one on one session. I speak on radio and television. My husband and I host a weekly podcast and we mentor couples via Riverside weekly. Yes, this once very insecure, overweight girl, with low self-esteem, is now thriving in an environment where she was born to belong; although, I must admit that I would have never picked this life for myself. From writing six books, sending out hundreds of press releases, holding radio interviews in my closet (to achieve excellent sound quality), and being told 'no' thousands of times, I can say with certainty that this is what I was created for.

The Power of Unpacking Your Why

If I have learned only one lesson worth sharing, it is the power of unpacking your "Why" before you invest in your how, which will save you and others priceless time. Why do I wake up each day not knowing the outcome, but still have hope and joy each day? It is my "Why". God loves me, and He loves everyone around me, even the people I did not know or like. God wants to use my mess, my pain, and my failures. All I must do is willingly give them to Him and He turns them into something beautiful. I hope my living God's life in the power of my unpacked "Why", encourages you to discover your why.

What do I mean by unpacked? I will give you an Illustration. For years, I lost and gained weight. I also had unresolved conflicts with people and did not know how to use my voice for good. I had to ask myself, "Why?" What is the common thread in these seemingly different events? Me. It is me! I cannot control anyone or anything around me.

My "Why" is for me. Why don't I use my power and energy to change me? Why don't I set boundaries, limits, and have realistic expectations for myself and others? Why don't I learn to say 'no' to myself and others? Why have I wasted so much time? Why can't I forgive? Why can't I ask for forgiveness? I asked myself, "Why?" until there were no whys left. I call this unpacking yourself. Our "Why" is the key to finding peace and solutions.

Today, I challenge you to use your choices in ways that serve you well and empower you to develop the strength to serve God and others. That is the success that brings hope, freedom, and liberty. We cannot pick our families of origin, our DNA, or even our facial features. We can control our time, our choices and our habits. We can examine them, manage them, and we must own them! Remember, we are more alike than we are different. You are not alone! Your story, your pain, and your difficulty are not unique. However, you are! And there is more to life than living for yourself alone.

Take the journey inward to get to know and love God, yourself, and others. Know and love your family and others. Be kind to yourself and others. Have dreams that are so big that they rattle your mind, causing you to need the help of others to accomplish them. Own and unpack your "Why." Know and trust that God has a good plan for your life filled with love, laughter, pain, disappointment, and purpose.

"I am more than enough in Christ Jesus." My name is Renée M. Beavers, and to look at me on the outside, I appear to be just like everyone else and I am like you. I like to stay honest, open, and transparent (H.O.T); it is how I thrive in relationships. You and I are more alike than we are different. If you asked how I became the person I am today, I would say I am a product of my choices and not just my environment alone. Our choices form our habits and our habits shape our lifestyles. Many of us have had our share of disappointment, sadness, heartbreak, and childhood of origin issues. Many of us have experienced rejection, betrayal, failure, and sickness. The five-million-dollar question is,

"What will we do with it all? Do we unpack it, or do we act as if we are Ok? The choice is ours to make, but the effects impact everyone. We have the same basic needs. Love, belonging, security, and purpose connects us to one another and God. Let us unpack the pain of our past together. It is weighing us down!

GIL & RENÉE BEAVERS

After years of serving in marriage ministry, Gil and Renée Beavers have come to understand that many marital challenges stem from unresolved issues that singles bring into their marriages. Recognizing this, they felt called to prepare singles for the journey of marriage by addressing the inner struggles and past pains they may carry. By helping singles identify their growth areas and strengths, they aim to instill confidence in themselves, making it easier to enter into marriage with assurance and self-awareness.

As the creators and stewards of Rich Relationships Refuge LLC, Gil and Renée draw on their more than thirty years of marriage and fifteen years of coaching experience to bridge the gap between engagement and marriage. They believe that marriage, often overlooked in ministry, deserves more attention, prompting them to launch the Rich Relationships Project.

Their book, "Singles Blueprint for Dating and Marriage," extends beyond mere text it's a community dedicated to applying biblical principles to real-life relationships. Drawing parallels between building a home and building a relationship, they share their experiences of owning and selling multiple homes, emphasizing the profound similarities between the two processes. With a focus on three key aspects The Foundation, The Framework, and The Code they guide singles through the journey of building strong, enduring relationships based on love rather than fear.

Through their work, Gil and Renée invite singles to embark on this transformative journey with them, offering guidance, support, and a roadmap to a fulfilling and lasting marriage.

Love,

Gil & Renée Beavers

TABLE OF CONTENTS

Chapter 5: "Enlightenment" and Becoming a Couple 33

Chapter 6: Practical Tips for Christ Centered Dating 41

Chapter 7: Overcoming Obstacles in Dating 49

Chapter 1

INTRODUCTION

Meet Gil J & Renée M Beavers: Your Marriage Mentors

Welcome, RICH readers, to the journey of a lifetime a journey toward finding and nurturing a love that reflects the very essence of Christ's love for His bride, the Church. We are Gil J and Renée M Beavers, honored to serve as your guides on this adventure with thirty-five years of love, friendship, and marriage under our belts. We are living proof that love and marriage can last and be fulfilling with Christ at the center of it all.

For nineteen years, we have dedicated our lives to helping couples navigate the terrain of relationships, dating, and married life. Our own journey has been a testament to the transformative power of God's love, guiding us through both the joys and challenges of married life.

As marriage mentors, we understand the importance of not only finding love but also cultivating a love that endures. We believe that every relationship has the potential to reflect the beauty of Christ's love when it is founded upon His principles and nurtured with intentionality and grace.

The Purpose of Dating: From Initial Attraction to Everlasting Commitment

In a world where dating has become synonymous with casual encounters and fleeting romances, it's crucial to revisit the true purpose of dating. Dating is not merely a means to pass the time or satisfy our desires for companionship; it is a sacred journey toward discovering God's plan for our lives and our relationships.

From the moment of initial attraction to the promise of everlasting commitment, dating offers us the opportunity to discern God's will for our future, to grow in self-awareness and maturity, and to honor Him in every aspect of our interactions with others.

Setting the Foundation: Christ Centered Approach to Dating

At the heart of our approach to dating lies a commitment to Christ centeredness. We believe that Christ should be the foundation upon which every relationship is built, guiding our thoughts, words, and actions as we seek to love and honor one another.

A Christ centered approach to dating is characterized by prayer, discernment, and a commitment to purity and integrity. It is rooted in the belief that God has a unique plan for each of us and that He delights in leading His children into relationships that reflect His perfect love.

Throughout this book, we will explore the principles of Christ centered dating, offering practical wisdom, biblical insights, and personal life lessons to guide you on your journey toward lasting love. Whether you are single and seeking a mate or currently in a relationship, we invite you to join us as we embark on this transformative adventure together.

Note: Throughout this book, we will use the names Jasmine and Marcus as Illustrations of real-world experiences. While the names are not real, the experiences they share are representative of the challenges and triumphs many couples face in their relationships.

W.A.Y.S

I am only responsible for how I choose to treat you! Not for how you choose to treat me. RMB

NOTES

_____
_____
_____
_____
_____
_____
_____
_____
_____
_____
_____
_____
_____
_____
_____
_____
_____
_____
_____
_____
_____
_____
_____

Chapter 2

UNDERSTANDING THE DIFFERENCE: GOING OUT VS. DATING WITH CLARITY AND INTENTIONALITY

Understanding the Dynamics

Going out, much like browsing through items in a store, encompasses casual interactions and spending time together without a definitive commitment to dating. It involves engaging in various activities, such as grabbing coffee, attending events, or hanging out with friends, in a relaxed and noncommittal manner. This form of socializing allows individuals to explore connections, share experiences, and get to know each other without the pressure of romantic expectations.

On the other hand, dating involves a deliberate and intentional commitment to building a meaningful relationship from the outset. It requires clarity, communication, and mutual understanding of each other's intentions and expectations. Unlike going out, where interactions may be spontaneous and informal, dating entails setting clear boundaries and establishing a rapport with the intention of pursuing a deeper connection and potentially a long-term relationship or marriage.

Illustrating the Difference

Consider the ILLUSTRATION of Marcus and Jazmine, who met through mutual friends at a social gathering. They enjoyed each other's company and found themselves spending time together frequently, whether it was grabbing lunch, attending concerts, or going for walks in the park. Their interactions were relaxed and enjoyable, characterized by shared laughter and meaningful conversations. While they appreciated each other's company and valued their growing, they were both aware that they were simply "going out" and exploring the possibility of a deeper connection without any explicit commitment to dating.

As their relationship progressed, Marcus and Jazmine began to realize that their feelings for each other were evolving beyond mere friendship. They found themselves drawn to each other in a deeper way and felt a strong desire to pursue a more meaningful connection. Recognizing the shift in their feelings, they engaged in open and honest conversations about their intentions and desires for the relationship. They expressed their mutual interest in exploring the potential for a romantic connection and agreed to enter into a dating relationship with the intention of getting to know each other on a deeper level and discerning whether they were compatible for a long-term commitment.

The Importance of Clarity and Intentionality

Understanding this distinction is crucial for maintaining clarity and integrity in relationships. It prevents misunderstandings and ensures that both individuals are on the same page regarding the nature and direction of their interactions. By discerning between going out and dating, individuals can approach relationships with intentionality, respect, and purpose.

Call to Action

1. Reflect on your past and current interactions with others. Have you been intentional about setting clear boundaries and expectations in your relationships?

2. Take inventory of your own intentions and desires when spending time with someone. Are you simply going out for fun, or are

you genuinely interested in pursuing a deeper connection?

3. Have honest conversations with potential mates about your intentions and expectations for the relationship. Be transparent about your feelings and desires, and listen actively to their perspective.

4. Seek guidance and wisdom from God as you navigate the complexities of dating and relationships. Pray for discernment and clarity in your interactions, trusting that God will guide you in His perfect will.

5. Commit to honoring God and respecting others in your relationships, whether they remain casual or evolve into something more serious. Treat each person with dignity, kindness, and love, reflecting the character of Christ in all your interactions.

6. Reflect on your current relationships or interactions. Are you simply "going out" with or pursuing a dating relationship.

7. Seek God's guidance and wisdom in discerning the nature of your relationships. Pray for clarity and discernment as you navigate the complexities of dating and relationships.

8. Commit to honoring God and respecting others in your interactions, whether you're simply going out or pursuing a dating relationship.

9. Take proactive steps to ensure that your relationships are grounded in honesty, integrity, and mutual respect, regardless of whether progress to dating or remain casual.

ILLUSTRATION

For Marcus, the distinction between casual interactions and intentional dating had always been a blurry one. He had often found himself going out with someone simply for the sake of companionship, without truly considering whether there was potential for a deeper connection. But as he delved into the teachings of Gil and Renée, Marcus began to understand the importance of clarity and intentionality in his dating life.

Jasmine, too, had struggled with the concept of intentional dating. In a world where casual hookups and superficial connections seemed to reign supreme, she had often felt pressure to conform to societal norms. But as she reflected on her own experiences and the insights shared by her mentors, Jasmine realized that true fulfillment could only come from dating with clarity and purpose, seeking out a life mate that aligned with her values and aspirations.

Chapter 2: Verse: "Do not conform to the pattern of this world, but be transformed by the renewing of your mind. Then you will be able to test and approve what God's will is his good, pleasing and perfect will." Romans 12:2 (NIV)

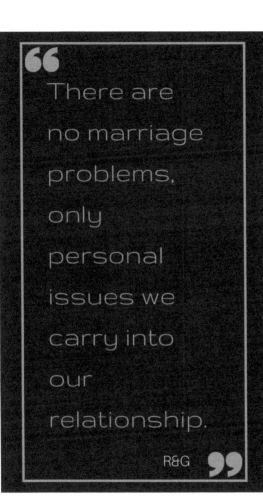

"There are no marriage problems, only personal issues we carry into our relationship.

R&G "

NOTES

_____

_____

_____

_____

_____

_____

_____

_____

_____

_____

_____

_____

_____

_____

_____

_____

_____

_____

_____

_____

_____

_____

Chapter 3

Initial Meeting/ Attraction

The Power of First Impressions: Making a Meaningful Connection

The journey of love often begins with a single moment a glance exchanged across a crowded room, a casual conversation that sparks something deeper, or a shared interest that ignites a sense of connection. These initial moments of attraction hold within them the power to shape the course of our relationships, setting the stage for the journey ahead.

As you navigate the waters of initial attraction, it's important to approach each encounter with intentionality and mindfulness. Remember that first impressions are not merely fleeting moments but opportunities to lay the foundation for meaningful connections. Take the time to truly see and appreciate the person before you, recognizing the inherent dignity and worth that they possess as a child of God.

Seeking God's Guidance in Choosing a Mate

In the midst of the excitement and anticipation that accompany the early stages of attraction, it's easy to lose sight of the importance of seeking God's guidance in choosing a mate. Yet, as followers of Christ, we are called to surrender our desires and plans to His will, trusting that He knows what is best for us.

Before embarking on a romantic relationship, take time to seek God's wisdom and discernment through prayer and reflection. Invite Him into the process of decision making, asking Him to guide your steps and illuminate the path before you. Trust that He will lead you to the person He has prepared for you, one who will complement and enhance your journey of faith.

Honoring God in Your Interactions: Establishing Boundaries from the Start

As you navigate the early stages of attraction, it's essential to honor God in your interactions with others by establishing clear boundaries from the start. While the world may encourage a casual approach to dating, as Christians, we are called to uphold the principles of purity, respect, and honor in all of our relationships.

Set boundaries that align with your values and beliefs, communicating them openly and honestly with the person you are getting to know. Whether it's refraining from physical intimacy until marriage or maintaining emotional boundaries to protect your heart, prioritize honoring God in every aspect of your interactions.

Remember that boundaries are not meant to restrict or hinder your relationship but rather to safeguard the sanctity of your journey toward lasting love. By honoring God in your interactions from the very beginning, you lay a solid foundation for a relationship rooted in faith, trust, and mutual respect.

As you embark on the adventure of initial attraction, may you be guided by the wisdom of God, grounded in the truth of His word, and empowered by the love that surpasses all understanding. Embrace the power of first impressions, seek God's guidance in choosing a mate, and honor Him in your interactions as you lay the groundwork for a relationship that glorifies His name.

ILLUSTRATION

It was a chance encounter at a local charity event that brought Marcus and Jasmine together. As they struck up a conversation, Marcus felt an instant connection with Jasmine a sense of familiarity and warmth that he hadn't experienced in a long time. But as he learned from Gil and Renée, initial attraction was just the beginning of the journey towards finding a life mate.

Jasmine, too, was drawn to Marcus from the moment they met. His kindness, humor, and genuine interest in her passions made her feel seen and valued in a way that was rare and special. But as she reflected on the insights shared on the RICH Relationships Refuge podcast, Jasmine understood that true compatibility went beyond surface level attraction it required shared values, mutual respect, and rooted in faith.

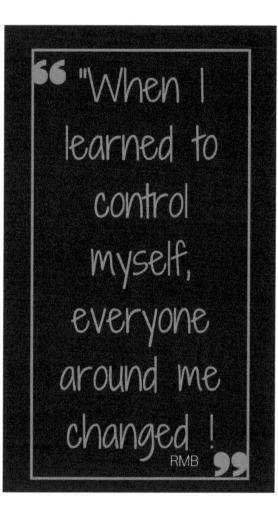

"When I learned to control myself, everyone around me changed !

RMB

Chapter 3: Initial Meeting/Attraction Verse

"Delight yourself in the Lord, and he will give you the desires of your heart." Psalm 37:4 (ESV) Call to Action: Seek God's guidance in every aspect of your relationship, including the initial stages of attraction. Delight in Him above all else, and trust that He will fulfill the desires of your heart according to His perfect plan.

NOTES

Chapter 4

CURIOSITY, INTEREST, AND INFATUATION

Navigating the Journey of Getting to Know Each Other

As initial attraction blossoms into curiosity and interest, the journey of getting to know each other begins in earnest. This phase is characterized by a sense of excitement and anticipation as you explore the depths of each other's personalities, values, and aspirations.

Navigating this journey requires patience, discernment, and a willingness to embrace vulnerability. Take the time to ask meaningful questions and listen attentively to the answers, seeking to understand the essence of who the other person is beyond surface level attributes.

Embrace opportunities for shared experiences and conversations that reveal the intricacies of your hearts and minds. Whether it's discussing your dreams for the future, sharing your favorite childhood memories, or simply enjoying each other's company, treasure these moments as building blocks for a deeper connection.

Building Emotional Intimacy: Sharing Your Heart with Wisdom

As you delve deeper into the journey of getting to know each other, emotional intimacy becomes a cornerstone of your relationship. Emotional intimacy is not merely about sharing your deepest thoughts and feelings but doing so with wisdom and discernment.

Be intentional about creating a safe space for vulnerability and authenticity in your relationship, where both mates feel valued, respected, and understood. Share your joys, fears, and struggles openly and honestly, knowing that true intimacy is born out of genuine transparency.

At the same time, exercise discernment in the timing and depth of your disclosures, honoring the pace of your relationship and respecting each other's boundaries. Remember that emotional intimacy is a journey that unfolds over time, deepening as trust and mutual understanding grow between you.

Recognizing the Signs of Infatuation vs. Genuine Interest

Amidst the excitement and emotional intensity of the journey of getting to know each other, it's important to discern between infatuation and genuine interest. Infatuation is characterized by a heightened sense of attraction and idealization, often leading to unrealistic expectations and impulsive decisions.

Genuine interest, on the other hand, is rooted in a deep appreciation for the other person's character, values, and personality. It is marked by a desire to truly understand and connect with the other person on a meaningful level, beyond superficial attractions.

Take time to reflect on your feelings and motivations, examining whether they stem from a place of genuine connection and compatibility or from the fleeting allure of infatuation. Seek counsel from trusted mentors and friends who can offer perspective and wisdom as you navigate this pivotal stage of your relationship.

By navigating the journey of curiosity, interest, and infatuation with intentionality and discernment, you lay a solid foundation for a relationship built on authenticity, trust, and mutual respect. Embrace the beauty of getting to know each other deeply, and trust that God will guide you every step of the way.

ILLUSTRATION

As Marcus and Jasmine continued to spend time together, they couldn't help but feel a growing sense of curiosity and interest towards each other. Marcus found himself captivated by Jasmine's intelligence and wit, while Jasmine admired Marcus's integrity and compassion. But as they navigated the early stages of their relationship, they also grappled with feelings of infatuation and uncertainty.

For Marcus, the line between genuine interest and infatuation had always been a blurry one. He had often found himself getting swept up in the excitement of a new relationship, only to realize later that his feelings were based more on fantasy than reality. But as he learned from the teachings of Gil and Renée, Marcus began to recognize the signs of infatuation and approach his budding relationship with Jasmine with a sense of clarity and discernment.

Jasmine, too, had experienced her fair share of infatuation in past relationships. She had been drawn to charismatic partners who seemed perfect on the surface, only to discover later that they lacked the depth and substance she craved. But as she reflected on her experiences and the insights shared by her mentors, Jasmine learned to differentiate between fleeting infatuation and genuine interest, approaching her relationship with Marcus with wisdom and self-awareness.

Chapter 4: Curiosity, Interest, and Infatuation Verse: "Above all, keep loving one another earnestly, since love covers a multitude of sins." 1 Peter 4:8 (ESV) Call to Action: Foster genuine love and curiosity for each other as you navigate the journey of getting to know one another. Love each other earnestly, covering any shortcomings with grace and compassion.

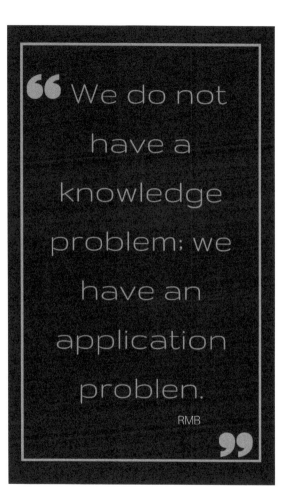

We do not have a knowledge problem; we have an application problem.

RMB

NOTES

Chapter 5

"ENLIGHTENMENT" AND BECOMING A COUPLE

Discovering Compatibility: Shared Values and Vision for the Future

As your relationship progresses beyond the initial stages of attraction and curiosity, you enter a phase of "enlightenment" a deeper understanding of each other's values, beliefs, and aspirations. This phase is marked by a growing sense of compatibility as you discover shared interests, goals, and vision for the future.

Take time to engage in meaningful conversations about your hopes, dreams, and priorities, exploring how they align with each other's and with God's plan for your lives. Identify areas of interest and compatibility, as well as potential areas of difference that may require further exploration and discussion.

Consider important aspects such as faith, family, career, and lifestyle preferences, recognizing that compatibility goes beyond mere surface level attractions. Seek God's guidance in discerning whether your relationship has the potential to flourish into a lifelong mate founded on shared values and vision.

Growing Together Spiritually: Strengthening Your Relationship with God as a Couple

As you journey toward becoming a couple, prioritize the cultivation of a strong spiritual foundation in your relationship. Growing together spiritually is essential for fostering a deep and enduring connection with each other and with God.

Make prayer, scripture study, and worship integral parts of your relationship, seeking opportunities to deepen your faith and understanding of God's word together. Attend church services, join small groups, and participate in spiritual practices that nourish your souls and draw you closer to God as a couple.

Support and encourage each other in your individual spiritual journeys, celebrating milestones and supporting each other through challenges. Allow your shared faith to serve as a source of strength, guidance, and inspiration as you navigate the joys and trials of life together.

Overcoming Challenges: Communication and Conflict Resolution in Dating

No relationship is without its challenges, and as you transition into becoming a couple, it's important to develop healthy communication and conflict resolution skills. Effective communication lays the groundwork for understanding, trust, and intimacy, while conflict resolution ensures that differences are addressed constructively and with respect.

Practice active listening, empathy, and vulnerability in your communication with each other, striving to understand each other's perspectives and feelings. Be willing to express your thoughts and emotions openly and honestly, while also being receptive to feedback and constructive criticism.

When conflicts arise, approach them with a spirit of humility and a commitment to finding mutually beneficial solutions. Focus on addressing the issue at hand rather than assigning blame or engaging in destructive behaviors. Remember that conflict can be an opportunity for growth and deeper understanding in your relationship.

By prioritizing shared values, growing together spiritually, and honing your communication and conflict resolution skills, you pave the way for a strong and resilient relationship. Embrace the journey of enlightenment as you discover compatibility, strengthen your spiritual bond, and overcome challenges together on the path toward becoming a couple united in love and faith.

ILLUSTRATION

As Marcus and Jasmine continued to explore their connection, they found themselves drawn closer together in heart and spirit. They spent hours talking about their dreams, their fears, and their shared values, finding comfort and solace in each other's presence. And as they grew in intimacy and understanding, they began to envision a future together a future built on love, trust, and mutual respect.

For Marcus, the journey towards enlightenment was one of self-discovery and revelation. As he opened his heart to Jasmine and shared his deepest hopes and fears, he felt a sense of liberation and empowerment that he had never experienced before. And as he learned from the teachings of Gil and Renée, Marcus understood that true enlightenment came not from external validation or material success, but from a deep and abiding connection with God and with others.

Jasmine, too, experienced a profound sense of enlightenment as she embarked on this new chapter of her life with Marcus. She felt a sense of clarity and purpose that she had never known before, as if all the pieces of her life were finally falling into place. And as she reflected on the teachings of the RICH Relationships Refuge, Jasmine understood that true enlightenment came from embracing her authentic self and aligning her life with God's plan for her.

Chapter 5: "Enlightenment" and Becoming a Couple Verse: "Therefore a man shall leave his father and his mother and hold fast to his, and they shall become one flesh." Genesis 2:24 (ESV) Call to Action: Commit to becoming one flesh in your relationship, prioritizing unity and mate as you journey toward becoming a couple united in Christ.

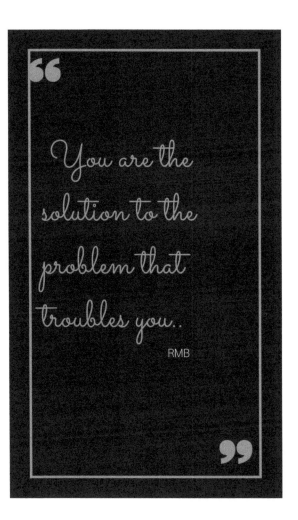

"

You are the
solution to the
problem that
troubles you..

RMB

"

Notes

Chapter 6

PRACTICAL TIPS FOR CHRIST CENTERED DATING

Setting Healthy Relationship Goals

In Christ centered dating, setting healthy relationship goals is essential for fostering growth, unity, and mutual respect. Begin by prayerfully considering your individual goals and desires for the relationship, and then come together to discuss and establish shared goals align with God's plan for your lives.

Consider setting goals related to communication, spiritual growth, and serving others as a couple. Commit to regular check-ins to assess your progress and make any necessary adjustments along the way. Remember that healthy relationship goals are not rigid expectations but flexible guidelines designed to support and strengthen your bond as a couple.

Dating with Integrity and Purity: Honoring God in Your Physical Boundaries

As followers of Christ, honoring God in your physical boundaries is paramount in Christ centered dating. Establish clear boundaries from the beginning of your relationship, and commit to upholding them with integrity and purity.

Communicate openly and honestly with each other about your expectations and boundaries regarding physical affection. Set limits that align with your values and convictions, and respect each other's boundaries with sensitivity and grace.

Pray for strength and guidance in resisting temptation, and seek accountability from trusted friends and mentors who can support you in your commitment to purity. Remember that physical intimacy is a precious gift from God, reserved for the covenant of marriage, and honor Him by preserving it for that sacred union.

Enjoying the Journey: Fun and Meaningful Activities for Couples

While the journey of Christ centered dating is marked by intentionality and spiritual growth, it is also important to prioritize enjoyment and fun as a couple. Take time to nurture your relationship through shared experiences and meaningful activities that bring you joy and strengthen your bond.

Explore shared interests and hobbies together, whether it's hiking in nature, cooking a meal together, or attending a concert or cultural event. Embrace opportunities for adventure and spontaneity, and cherish the moments of laughter and connection that arise along the way.

Prioritize quality time together, free from distractions and outside pressures, to deepen your emotional intimacy and build lasting memories. Create rituals and traditions that are meaningful to you as a couple, whether it's a weekly date night, a monthly getaway, or an annual pilgrimage to a special place.

By setting healthy relationship goals, honoring God in your physical boundaries, and enjoying the journey together, you cultivate a Christ centered dating experience that is both enriching and fulfilling. Embrace the adventure of dating with joy and gratitude, trusting that God is guiding your steps and blessing your relationship with His abundant love and grace.

ILLUSTRATION

As Marcus and Jasmine embarked on their Christ centered dating journey, they eagerly embraced practical tips to nurture and strengthen their relationship. They recognized that building a healthy and God honoring partnership required intentional effort and commitment. Setting aside dedicated time for prayer and reflection became a cornerstone of their relationship. Each day, they would come together to seek God's guidance, wisdom, and blessing upon their journey.

Communication played a vital role in Marcus and Jasmine's relationship. They prioritized open and honest dialogue, creating a safe space for sharing their thoughts, feelings, and aspirations. By actively listening to each other and expressing themselves authentically, they deepened their connection and fostered mutual understanding.

In addition to spiritual practices, Marcus and Jasmine enjoyed engaging in meaningful activities together. They found joy in attending church events, volunteering in their community, and participating in group Bible studies. These shared experiences not only strengthened their bond but also allowed them to grow spiritually as individuals and as a couple.

Marcus and Jasmine also recognized the importance of setting healthy boundaries in their relationship. They discussed their values, beliefs, and expectations openly, ensuring that their actions aligned with their convictions. By respecting each other's boundaries and honoring God in their interactions, they cultivated a relationship built on trust, respect, and integrity.

As they navigated the complexities of modern dating, Marcus and Jasmine leaned on the wisdom of their mentors and the support of their community. They sought guidance from married couples who had walked the path before them, gleaning insights and advice from their experiences. With humility and a willingness to learn, they embraced the opportunity to grow and mature in their relationship.

Chapter 6: Practical Tips for Christ Centered Dating Verse: "And let us consider how to stir up one another to love and good works." Hebrews 10:24 (ESV) Call to Action: Encourage and uplift each other in your relationship, striving to stir up love and good works in each other's lives. Be intentional about nurturing your relationship and growing in love and righteousness together.

"You can't know what you don't know! Instead of guessing, it's best to get a test." RMB

NOTES

Chapter 7

OVERCOMING
OBSTACLES IN DATING

Dealing with Rejection and Disappointment

In the journey of dating, rejection and disappointment are inevitable obstacles that can test our faith and resilience. Whether it's a relationship that doesn't progress as hoped or a rejection from someone we care about, it's important to navigate these challenges with grace and trust in God's plan.

Allow yourself to acknowledge and process your feelings of disappointment and hurt, but don't let them define your worth or diminish your hope for the future. Remember that God's love for you is unchanging and unconditional, and His plans for you are good, even in the face of rejection.

Seek comfort and support from trusted friends, family members, and mentors who can offer encouragement and perspective during difficult times. Lean on your faith in God's sovereignty and trust that He is working all things together for your good, even when circumstances seem bleak.

Handling outside Influences: Family, Friends, and Cultural Expectations

Navigating the complexities of dating often involves contending with outside influences such as family, friends, and cultural expectations. While these influences can provide valuable insight and support, they can also present challenges and conflicts that test the strength of your relationship.

Set healthy boundaries with family and friends, communicating openly and respectfully about your relationship and your desire for their support. Seek to balance their input with your own discernment and convictions, trusting that ultimately, you and your mate know what is best for your relationship.

Be mindful of cultural expectations and societal pressures that may influence your dating journey, but don't let them dictate your decisions or define your worth. Stay grounded in your faith and values, and prioritize the voice of God above all others as you navigate the complexities of dating in today's world.

Trusting God's Timing: Patience and Perseverance in the Dating Season

One of the greatest challenges in dating is trusting God's timing, especially when it seems like everyone around you is finding love except for you. However, God's timing is perfect, and He has a unique plan for each of us that unfolds in His own time and way.

Cultivate patience and perseverance as you wait for God to reveal His plan for your relationship. Trust that He is working behind the scenes, orchestrating divine connections and preparing you and your mate for the journey ahead.

Use this season of waiting as an opportunity for growth and self-discovery, focusing on deepening your relationship with God and becoming the best version of yourself. Stay open to His leading and guidance, and be willing to step out in faith when He calls you to take action.

By dealing with rejection and disappointment with grace, handling outside influences with wisdom and discernment, and trusting God's timing with patience and perseverance, you can overcome obstacles in dating and emerge stronger and more resilient than ever before. Embrace the journey with faith and hope, knowing that God is with you every step of the way, leading you toward a future filled with His blessings and grace.

ILLUSTRATION

Marcus and Jasmine's journey was not without its challenges. Like any couple, they encountered obstacles along the way that tested their resolve and commitment to each other. From misunderstandings and disagreements to external pressures and societal expectations, they faced adversity with courage and faith.

When conflicts arose, Marcus and Jasmine approached them with humility and grace. They recognized that disagreements were a natural part of any relationship and an opportunity for growth and reconciliation. By practicing active listening, empathy, and forgiveness, they were able to navigate through challenges with understanding and compassion.

At times, Marcus and Jasmine found themselves grappling with doubts and insecurities. They questioned whether they were on the right path or if their relationship was meant to be. In those moments of uncertainty, they turned to prayer and sought guidance from their mentors and trusted friends. Through reflection and introspection, they gained clarity and perspective, reaffirming their commitment to each other and to God's plan for their lives.

External pressures also posed challenges for Marcus and Jasmine. They faced scrutiny and judgment from others who questioned their choices or doubted the strength of their relationship. However, they remained steadfast in their faith and confidence in each other, refusing to let outside opinions dictate their journey. With resilience and determination, they stood firm in their commitment to love and honor each other, regardless of the obstacles they faced.

Chapter 7: Overcoming Obstacles in Dating Verse: "I can do all things through him who strengthens me." Philippians 4:13 (ESV) Call to Action: Lean on God's strength and grace as you overcome obstacles in your relationship. Trust in His power to guide you through challenges and to provide the wisdom and courage you need to persevere.

> An appetite driven life leads to regret! It's ok to say no!
>
> RMB

NOTES

Chapter 8

THE ROLE OF
COMMUNITY IN YOUR
RELATIONSHIP

Surrounding Yourself with Supportive Friends and Family

In the journey of a Christ centered relationship, the support of friends and family can be a source of strength, encouragement, and wisdom. Surround yourself with individuals who genuinely care about you and your relationship, and who will uplift and support you in your journey toward lasting love.

Share your joys, challenges, and milestones with your loved ones, allowing them to celebrate with you and provide a shoulder to lean on during difficult times. Lean on their wisdom and experience as you navigate the complexities of relationships, and cherish the bonds of love and friendship that sustain you along the way.

Finding a Christ Centered Community: Church, Small Groups, and Fellowship

A Christ centered community is an invaluable resource for couples seeking to strengthen their relationship and grow in their faith together. Engage actively in your church community, attending services, participating in small groups, and joining fellowship opportunities that nurture your spiritual growth as a couple.

Surround yourselves with likeminded individuals who share your values and priorities, and who will support and encourage you in your journey of faith and love. Seek out mentors and couples who exemplify Christ centered relationships, learning from their experiences and seeking their guidance as you navigate the challenges and joys of dating and marriage.

Make community a priority in your relationship, investing time and energy into building meaningful connections and fostering mutual support and accountability. Embrace opportunities for service and ministry together, allowing your relationship to be a beacon of Christ's love and grace to those around you.

Seeking Wise Counsel: The Value of Mentors and Marriage Coaches

In addition to the support of friends and family, seek out wise counsel from mentors and marriage coaches who can offer guidance, perspective, and encouragement in your relationship. These individuals have walked the path before you and can provide invaluable insights and wisdom as you navigate the complexities of dating and marriage.

Be open to receiving feedback and advice, recognizing that the insights of others can help you grow and strengthen your relationship. Seek out mentors who share your faith and values, and who have a heart for helping couples thrive in their relationships.

Invest in premarital counseling and coaching to prepare for marriage, addressing important topics and challenges that may arise in your relationship. Embrace the opportunity to learn and grow together, and trust that God will use the guidance of wise counselors to bless and enrich your relationship.

By surrounding yourselves with supportive friends and family, engaging in a Christ centered community, and seeking wise counsel from mentors and marriage coaches, you strengthen the foundation of your relationship and ensure that it continues to flourish and thrive in the years to come. Embrace the blessings of community and fellowship, knowing that you are not alone on this journey of love and faith.

Surrounded by a supportive community, Marcus and Jasmine found strength and encouragement in their relationships with family, friends, and mentors. They recognized the importance of building a strong support network that would uplift and empower them on their journey towards marriage.

ILLUSTRATION

Marcus and Jasmine actively sought out opportunities to connect with likeminded individuals who shared their values and beliefs.

They attended church together, joined small groups, and participated in community events, fostering meaningful relationships and deepening their sense of belonging. These connections provided them with a sense of camaraderie and solidarity, reminding them that they were not alone in their journey.

In times of joy and celebration, Marcus and Jasmine's community rallied around them, rejoicing in their love and offering words of encouragement and blessing. Whether it was an engagement party, bridal shower, or wedding ceremony, their loved ones stood by their side, affirming their commitment to each other and to God.

But perhaps most importantly, Marcus and Jasmine's community served as a source of wisdom and guidance, offering counsel and support when they needed it most. They turned to their mentors and experienced couples for advice and encouragement, learning from their wisdom and drawing strength from their With humility and gratitude, they embraced the role of community in their relationship, recognizing that they were stronger together than they could ever be alone.

Chapter 8: The Role of Community in Your Relationship Verse: "Two are better than one, because they have a good reward for their toil." Ecclesiastes 4:9 (ESV) Call to Action: Embrace the support and encouragement of your community as you navigate your relationship. Seek guidance and accountability from trusted friends, family, and mentors who will walk alongside you in your journey of faith and love.

NOTES

Chapter 9

RED FLAGS AND WARNING SIGNS IN DATING

Recognizing Destructive Patterns: Emotional, Verbal, and Physical Abuse

In the journey of dating, it's essential to recognize and address red flags and warning signs that may indicate the presence of destructive patterns, such as emotional, verbal, or physical abuse. These behaviors are harmful and have no place in a Christ centered relationship.

Be vigilant in identifying signs of manipulation, control, or coercion in your relationship, and take action to address them promptly and decisively. Pay attention to how your mate communicates with you and treats you, and trust your instincts if something feels off or uncomfortable.

Know that you are not alone and that help is available if you find yourself in a situation where you are experiencing abuse. Reach out to trusted friends, family members, or professionals who can provide support and guidance, and seek resources and assistance from organizations dedicated to helping victims of abuse.

Understanding Your Worth in Christ: Setting Healthy Standards for Your Relationship

As a child of God, you are precious and deserving of love, respect, and dignity in your relationships. Understanding your worth in Christ is essential for setting healthy standards and boundaries in your dating life.

Take time to reflect on your values, beliefs, and priorities, and establish clear boundaries that align with your worth and identity in Christ. Communicate your standards openly and assertively with your mate, and be prepared to enforce them if necessary.

Remember that you have the right to be treated with kindness, honor, and respect in your relationship, and don't settle for anything less than God's best for you. Surround yourself with individuals who uplift and affirm your worth, and seek relationships that honor and reflect the love of Christ.

Trusting Your Instincts: When to Seek Guidance and Intervention

Trusting your instincts is crucial in recognizing and responding to red flags and warning signs in dating. If something feels wrong or unsettling in your relationship, don't ignore or dismiss your instincts listen to them and take action to address any concerns that arise.

Be proactive in seeking guidance and intervention if you find yourself in a situation where you feel unsafe or uncomfortable. Reach out to trusted friends, family members, or professionals who can provide support and assistance, and don't hesitate to seek help from authorities or organizations dedicated to addressing abuse and violence.

Remember that you are not alone in your journey, and there are people and resources available to help you navigate challenging situations. Trust in God's guidance and protection, and have faith that He will lead you to safety and healing as you seek to honor Him in your relationships.

By recognizing red flags and warning signs, understanding your worth in Christ, and trusting your instincts, you empower yourself to create healthy and thriving relationships that honor God and reflect His love and grace. Embrace the journey of growth and discernment, knowing that

God is with you every step of the way, guiding and protecting you as you seek His best for your life.

ILLUSTRATION

As Marcus and Jasmine navigated the complexities of dating, they remained vigilant in recognizing red flags and warning signs that could indicate potential problems in their relationship. They understood that discernment was essential in protecting their hearts and ensuring that they were on the right path.

They paid attention to inconsistencies in behavior and communication, recognizing that they could be indicators of deeper issues within the relationship. They also listened to their intuition, trusting their gut instincts when something felt off or out of alignment. By staying attuned to these warning signs, Marcus and Jasmine were able to address concerns early on and take proactive steps to safeguard their relationship.

Marcus and Jasmine also sought guidance from their mentors and trusted advisors when they encountered red flags in their relationship. They valued the perspectives of those who had walked the path before them, drawing upon their wisdom and experience to gain clarity and insight. With humility and a willingness to learn, they approached these conversations with openness and receptivity, knowing that their mentors had their best interests at heart.

But perhaps most importantly, Marcus and Jasmine remained grounded in their faith throughout their dating journey. They sought God's guidance and direction in their relationship, trusting that He would lead them on the right path. By staying rooted in prayer and Scripture, they found strength and assurance, knowing that God was with them every step of the way.

Chapter 10: Red Flags and Warning Signs in Dating Verse: "Be soberminded; be watchful. Your adversary the devil prowls around like a roaring lion, seeking someone to devour." 1 Peter

5:8 (ESV) Call to Action: Stay alert and discerning in your dating relationships, being vigilant against red flags and warning signs of destructive patterns. Guard your heart and mind against the schemes of the enemy, and seek wisdom and discernment from God as you navigate your relationships.

10 Red flags in the early stages of dating to look out for

In the early stages of dating, it's important to be observant for signs that might indicate potential problems or incompatibilities in the relationship. Here are 10 red flags to look out for:

1. Lack of Communication: If your date is consistently difficult to reach or doesn't respond promptly to messages, it could indicate a lack of interest or commitment.

2. Inconsistent Behavior: Watch out for inconsistencies in their behavior, such as canceling plans frequently or

being hot and cold in their interactions with you.

3. Disrespectful Behavior: Any signs of disrespect towards you, whether it's making rude remarks, disregarding your boundaries, or treating you poorly in public or private settings, should not be ignored.

4. Talking Only About Themselves: If your date dominates conversations and shows little interest in getting to know you or asking about your life, it may indicate self-centeredness or a lack of genuine interest in building a connection.

5. Avoidance of Personal Topics: Someone who avoids discussing personal topics or seems evasive when you ask questions about their past, interests, or goals may be hiding something or not ready to open up.

6. Overly Possessive or Jealous Behavior: Jealousy and

possessiveness, especially in the early stages of dating, can be warning signs of controlling behavior or insecurity that may escalate over time.

7. Unwillingness to Compromise: If your date consistently insists on having things their way and shows little willingness to compromise or consider your perspective, it could be a sign of selfishness or an inability to work together as a team.

8. Negative Attitude or Pessimism: Constant negativity or pessimism can be draining and may indicate underlying issues such as low self-esteem or a lack of emotional resilience.

9. History of Unhealthy Relationships: Pay attention to any patterns of behavior or stories your date shares about past relationships that suggest they have a history of toxicity, abuse, or instability.

10. **Pressure for Commitment Too Soon:** Be cautious if your date pressures you for a commitment or tries to rush the progression of the relationship before you feel ready. Healthy relationships evolve naturally over time, and it's important to take things at a pace that feels comfortable for both parties.

Remember that one red flag on its own might not necessarily be a dealbreaker, but if you notice multiple warning signs or a pattern of concerning behavior, it's essential to trust your instincts and consider whether the relationship is worth pursuing further.

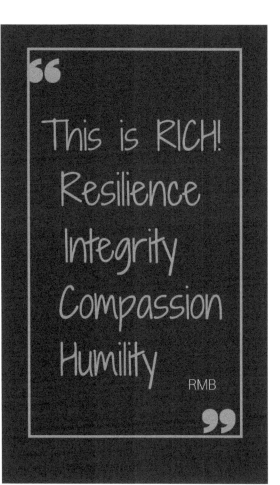

> " This is RICH!
> Resilience
> Integrity
> Compassion
> Humility "
>
> RMB

NOTES

Chapter 10

COMMITMENT OR ENGAGEMENT

Discerning God's Will: Seeking Confirmation for a Lifelong Mate

As your relationship deepens and matures, the time may come to discern God's will regarding a lifelong commitment. This pivotal stage requires prayer, discernment, and a willingness to surrender your plans and desires to God's perfect timing and guidance.

Seek confirmation from God through prayer, scripture, and seeking counsel from trusted mentors and spiritual advisors. Pay attention to the inner promptings of the Holy Spirit and the signs that God may be placing in your path, guiding you toward His perfect plan for your relationship.

Consider important factors such as compatibility, shared values, and mutual commitment to Christ as you discern whether your relationship is ready for the next step of commitment or engagement. Trust that God's timing is perfect, and He will reveal His will for your relationship in His own time and way.

Preparing for Marriage: Building a Solid Foundation Together

As you prepare for marriage, it's essential to lay a solid foundation for your future together. This foundation is built upon a commitment to Christ, mutual respect, trust, and a shared vision for your life as a couple.

Invest time and effort into premarital counseling and preparation, seeking guidance from experienced mentors and marriage counselors who can help you navigate potential challenges and strengthen your relationship. Address important topics such as communication, conflict resolution, finances, and roles within marriage, ensuring that you are both on the same page and prepared for the journey ahead.

Cultivate habits of prayer, study, and worship as a couple, inviting God to be the center of your relationship and guiding your steps as you prepare for marriage. Take time to build intimacy and connection through shared experiences, traditions, and rituals that reflect your values and priorities as a couple.

The Importance of Accountability and Mentorship in the Dating Process

Throughout the dating process and as you prepare for marriage, accountability and mentorship play a crucial role in guiding and supporting your relationship. Surround yourselves with wise and experienced mentors who can offer guidance, wisdom, and accountability as you navigate the complexities of relationships and marriage.

Seek out couples who exemplify Christ centered love and commitment, learning from their experiences and seeking their counsel as you prepare for marriage. Be open to receiving feedback and advice, recognizing that the insights of others can help you grow and strengthen your relationship.

Stay connected to your community of faith, participating in small groups, Bible studies, and fellowship opportunities that provide support and encouragement for your relationship. Foster friendships with other couples who share your values and priorities, journeying alongside each other as you navigate the joys and challenges of relationships and marriage.

By discerning God's will, preparing for marriage, and seeking accountability and mentorship, you lay a strong foundation for a lifelong mate rooted in faith, love, and commitment. Embrace the journey of commitment and engagement with confidence, knowing that God is guiding your steps and preparing you for a future filled with His blessings and grace.

ILLUSTRATION

As Marcus and Jasmine's relationship continued to flourish, they found themselves at a pivotal moment: the decision to commit to a lifelong partnership through engagement. This significant step required careful consideration, prayerful discernment, and a deep understanding of God's will for their lives.

For Marcus, the prospect of proposing to Jasmine was both exhilarating and daunting. He knew that asking her to be his wife meant committing to a lifetime of love, sacrifice, and partnership. As he pondered this decision, Marcus sought guidance from his mentors, reflecting on the qualities that made Jasmine the perfect mate for him. He admired her strength, her kindness, and her unwavering faith in God, knowing that she was the woman he wanted to spend the rest of his life with.

Jasmine, too, wrestled with the weight of Marcus's proposal. She felt a surge of joy and gratitude at the thought of becoming his life mate, but she also understood the gravity of the commitment they were about to make. As she prayed and sought wisdom from her mentors, Jasmine reflected on the depth of her love for Marcus and the shared vision they had for their future together. She knew that saying yes to his proposal meant embarking on a journey of growth, adventure, and companionship a journey she was eager to undertake with him by her side.

Before taking the leap into engagement, Marcus and Jasmine took deliberate steps to ensure they were aligning their decision with

God's will. They spent time in prayer, seeking His guidance and direction for their relationship. They also sought counsel from their mentors, drawing on their wisdom and experience to gain clarity and perspective.

As Marcus prepared to propose, he wanted to ensure that the foundation of their relationship was built on a solid bedrock of faith, trust, and mutual respect. He planned a romantic and heartfelt proposal, pouring out his love for Jasmine and expressing his commitment to cherish and honor her for the rest of their lives. With a ring in hand and a heart full of love, Marcus dropped to one knee and asked Jasmine to be his life mate. Overwhelmed with emotion, Jasmine said yes, knowing in her heart that she was making the right decision.

With their engagement, Marcus and Jasmine embarked on a new chapter of their relationship one filled with excitement, anticipation, and preparation for marriage. They knew that this journey would not be without its challenges, but they were confident that with God's grace and the support of their community, they would navigate the joys and trials of married life together.

As they shared the news of their engagement with family and friends, Marcus and Jasmine were filled with gratitude and joy, knowing that they were embarking on a journey ordained by God. They looked forward to the adventure ahead, trusting in His plan for their lives and eager to build a future filled with love, laughter, and lasting commitment.

Chapter 10: Commitment or Engagement Verse: "Commit your work to the Lord, and your plans will be established." Proverbs 16:3 (ESV) Call to Action: Surrender your relationship to the Lord, trusting in His plan for your future together. Commit your desires and intentions to Him, and He will establish your plans according to His perfect will.

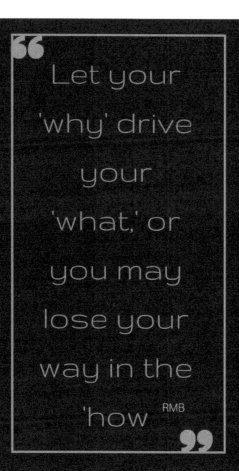

Let your 'why' drive your 'what,' or you may lose your way in the 'how RMB

NOTES

Chapter 11

EMBRACING GOD'S
DESIGN FOR MARRIAGE

The Beauty of Covenant Love:
Reflections on Christ and His Bride

Marriage is a sacred covenant ordained by God, reflecting the profound love and commitment between Christ and His bride, the Church. Just as Christ sacrificially gave Himself for His bride, husbands and wives are called to love and honor each other in a covenant of mutual devotion and fidelity.

Embrace the beauty of covenant love in your marriage, recognizing it as a reflection of God's unfailing love and faithfulness. Cherish the sacred bond that unites you and your spouse, and strive to nurture and protect it with steadfast devotion and commitment.

Serving Each Other in Love: The Role of Sacrifice and Selflessness in Marriage

Central to God's design for marriage is the call to serve one another in love, following the ILLUSTRATION of Christ who humbly served His disciples and ultimately laid down His life for them. In marriage, sacrificial love and selflessness are the cornerstones of a thriving and fulfilling relationship.

Commit to serving and honoring your spouse with humility and grace, seeking their welfare and happiness above your own. Be quick to forgive, slow to anger, and eager to extend compassion and kindness in all circumstances.

Embrace a spirit of unity and mate in your marriage, working together as a team to overcome challenges and celebrate victories. Value each other's strengths and weaknesses, and support and encourage each other in your individual growth and development.

A Lifetime of Growth and Adventure: Embracing the Journey Together

Marriage is a journey of growth, adventure, and discovery a shared pilgrimage toward becoming the people God created us to be. Embrace the journey together with open hearts and minds, eager to learn and grow in love and wisdom each day.

Commit to cultivating a culture of continuous growth and improvement in your marriage, seeking opportunities for spiritual, emotional, and relational development. Invest time and energy into nurturing your relationship, through shared experiences, meaningful conversations, and intentional acts of love and service.

Embrace the adventure of marriage with courage and faith, knowing that God is with you every step of the way, guiding and sustaining you through every season of life. Celebrate the joys, navigate the challenges, and cherish the moments of laughter, love, and connection that enrich your journey together.

By embracing God's design for marriage, you honor the sacred covenant of love and commitment that unites you and your spouse. May your marriage be a testament to the beauty of God's design, a beacon of hope and inspiration to all who witness the transformative power of covenant love lived out in faithful obedience to His will.

ILLUSTRATION

For Marcus and Jasmine, the journey towards marriage was not merely a union between two individuals but a covenant blessed by God. As they approached this sacred commitment, they embarked on a profound exploration of God's design for marriage, seeking to align their hearts and lives with His divine plan.

Central to their understanding of marriage was the recognition that it was a reflection of the unconditional love and sacrificial relationship between Christ and His church. Marcus and Jasmine embraced this biblical truth wholeheartedly, viewing their union as a testament to God's faithfulness and grace. They understood that their love for each other was a gift from God, to be cherished and nurtured for a lifetime.

As they prepared to exchange vows, Marcus and Jasmine reflected on the foundational principles of marriage outlined in Scripture. They recognized the importance of mutual submission and selflessness, committing to serve each other with humility and grace. They understood that their relationship was not just about their individual happiness but about building a partnership that honored God and brought glory to His name.

Marcus and Jasmine also embraced the concept of unity in marriage, recognizing that they were called to become one flesh in every aspect of their lives. They committed to sharing their dreams, their joys, and their sorrows, walking hand in hand through the journey of life. They understood that true intimacy was not just physical but emotional, spiritual, and relational, as they sought to deepen their connection with each other and with God.

But perhaps most importantly, Marcus and Jasmine embraced the covenantal nature of marriage, pledging to love and honor each other in sickness and in health, for better or for worse, until death do them part. They understood that marriage was not just a contract but a sacred covenant before God, requiring unwavering commitment and fidelity.

As they stood before God and their loved ones on their wedding day, Marcus and Jasmine exchanged vows that reflected the depth of their commitment and the sincerity of their love. They promised to support and encourage each other, to laugh together in times of joy, and to lean on each other in times of sorrow. They vowed to honor God in their marriage, seeking His guidance and strength as they embarked on this new chapter of their lives together.

As they celebrated their union with family and friends, Marcus and Jasmine were filled with gratitude and humility, knowing that their love was a gift from God. They embraced the beauty of covenantal love, rejoicing in the privilege of sharing their lives with each other. And as they looked towards the future, they did so with hope and anticipation, trusting in God's faithfulness to guide them on their journey as husband and wife.

Chapter 11: Embracing God's Design for Marriage Verse: "Therefore a man shall leave his father and his mother and hold fast to his wife, and the two shall become one flesh." Ephesians 5:31 (ESV) Call to Action: Embrace God's design for marriage, holding fast to each other in love and unity. Commit to building a Christ centered marriage that reflects the beauty and sanctity of the union between Christ and His bride, the Church.

NOTES

Chapter 12

CONCLUSION

Reflecting on Your Dating Journey: Gratitude and Lessons Learned

As you reach the conclusion of this book, take a moment to reflect on your dating journey with gratitude and humility. Consider the lessons you've learned, the growth you've experienced, and the blessings you've encountered along the way.

Give thanks for the relationships that have shaped and enriched your life, whether they led to lasting love or valuable lessons. Embrace the challenges and setbacks as opportunities for growth and refinement, trusting that God works all things together for good for those who love Him.

Looking Ahead with Hope: Trusting God's Plan for Your Future Together

As you look ahead to the future with hope and anticipation, trust in God's plan for your relationship and your lives together. Surrender your hopes, dreams, and desires to His will, knowing that He is faithful to guide and direct your steps according to His perfect purpose.

Embrace the journey ahead with courage and faith, knowing that God is with you every step of the way, leading and guiding you toward a future filled with hope and promise. Keep your eyes fixed on Him as you navigate the joys and challenges of dating, marriage, and beyond.

Becoming Ambassadors of Christ Centered Love: Sharing Your Story with Others

As you continue on your journey of Christ centered love, consider the impact of your relationship on those around you. Become ambassadors of God's love and grace, sharing your story with others as a testimony to His faithfulness and goodness.

Invite others into the beauty of Christ centered relationships, demonstrating through your words and actions the transformative power of love rooted in faith and commitment. Serve as a beacon of hope and encouragement to those who may be struggling in their own relationships, offering support, guidance, and prayer.

By sharing your story with others, you become instruments of God's love and grace, shining His light into the darkness and pointing others toward the source of true fulfillment and joy. May your relationship be a testament to the glory of God and a reflection of His love to all who cross your path?

ILLUSTRATION

As Marcus and Jasmine approached the conclusion of their dating journey, they took time to reflect on the experiences, growth, and blessings that had shaped their relationship. This chapter was a moment of introspection a chance to express gratitude for the journey they had shared and to glean valuable lessons for the future.

For Marcus, the reflection process began with a heart full of gratitude. He looked back on the moments of connection, laughter, and love that had defined their relationship, feeling overwhelmed by the goodness of God's provision. He appreciated the way Jasmine had enriched his life, challenging him to grow, and inspiring him to be a better man. Marcus recognized the significance of their journey, acknowledging that every twist and turn had led them closer to each other and to God.

Jasmine, too, felt a deep sense of gratitude as she reflected on their dating journey. She marveled at the way God had orchestrated their paths to intersect, guiding them towards each other with love and grace. Jasmine cherished the memories they had created together, from quiet moments of conversation to adventures in new places. She felt blessed to have Marcus by her side, knowing that their relationship was a gift she would always treasure.

But amidst the gratitude, Marcus and Jasmine also recognized the importance of learning from their dating experiences. They took stock of the challenges they had faced the misunderstandings, the disagreements, the moments of doubt and saw them as opportunities for growth. They acknowledged their mistakes and shortcomings, seeking forgiveness and extending grace to each other as they navigated the complexities of relationships.

One of the most valuable lessons Marcus and Jasmine gleaned from their dating journey was the importance of communication. They realized that open and honest dialogue was essential for building trust, resolving conflicts, and deepening intimacy. They committed to listening to each other with empathy and understanding, recognizing that true connection required vulnerability and authenticity.

Another lesson they learned was the significance of patience and perseverance in relationships. Marcus and Jasmine understood that love was not always easy that it required effort, sacrifice, and a willingness to weather the storms together. They embraced the challenges of dating with resilience and determination, trusting in God's timing and His plan for their lives.

As Marcus and Jasmine concluded their reflection, they did so with hearts full of gratitude and minds enriched with wisdom. They recognized that their dating journey had been more than just a series of romantic moments it had been a transformative experience that had shaped their hearts and souls in profound ways. And as they looked towards the future, they did so with hope and anticipation, trusting that God would continue to guide them on their journey of love and faith.

In the end, Marcus and Jasmine understood that their dating journey was not just about finding a life mate it was about discovering themselves, growing in faith, and embracing the beauty of God's plan for their lives. And as they stepped into the next chapter of their relationship, they did so with gratitude for the past, excitement for the future, and a deep and abiding love for each other.

Chapter 12: Conclusion Verse: "And we know that for those who love God all things work together for good, for those who are called according to his purpose." Romans 8:28 (ESV) Call to Action: Trust in God's sovereignty and goodness as you reflect on your dating journey and look ahead to the future. Commit to living according to His purpose for your relationship, knowing that He works all things together for your ultimate good and His glory.

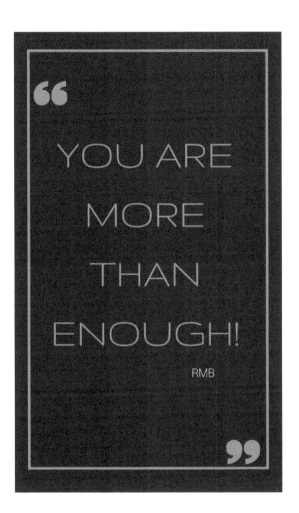

NOTES

APPENDIX

- ◆ Discussion Questions for Couples: Reflective questions to deepen your understanding of the principles discussed in this book and facilitate meaningful conversations with your mate.

- ◆ Recommended Reading List for Further Growth: A curated list of books and resources to support your continued growth and development in your relationship and faith journey.

♦ Resources for Seeking Counseling and Support: Information and contact details for organizations and professionals offering counseling and support services for couples seeking guidance and assistance in their relationship.

Discussion Questions for Couples:

1. Reflect on your dating journey together. What have been some of the highlights and challenges you've experienced?

2. How has your relationship grown spiritually since you first started dating? What practices or habits have helped nurture your faith as a couple?

3. Discuss your individual and shared goals for the future. How do your aspirations align, and how do you plan to support each other in achieving them?

4. How do you handle disagreements and conflicts in your relationship? What strategies have been effective in fostering understanding and resolution?

5. Reflect on the role of community in your relationship. How have friends, family, and mentors supported and influenced your journey together?

6. How do you prioritize quality time and intimacy in your relationship? What activities or rituals do you enjoy doing together to deepen your connection?

7. Discuss your approach to setting boundaries and maintaining purity in your relationship. How do you honor God in your physical and emotional interactions with each other?

8. Reflect on the concept of sacrificial love and service in your relationship. In what ways do you demonstrate

selflessness and humility toward each other?

9. How do you handle outside influences and cultural expectations in your relationship? How do you maintain unity and solidarity as a couple in the face of external pressures?

10. Reflect on your individual roles and responsibilities within the relationship. How do you support and complement each other in fulfilling these roles?

YOUR RICH MARRIAGE IS IN YOUR HANDS

MARRIAGE MENTORS is a groundbreaking mobile application, offering a streamlined and accessible platform to foster connections with God, yourself, and your current or prospective spouse.

WANT TO DOWNLOAD THE REALLY GREAT APP?

CHRIST-CENTERED

Marriage Mentors is more than just an app, it's a guiding light on your journey towards building a fulfilling and lasting marriage rooted in faith and centered on Christ.

COMMUNICATION BUILDING

Start by assessing your communication skills and understanding your readiness for marriage with our interactive assessments.

COMMUNITY- SUPPORT

Users can engage in meaningful introspection, identify areas for growth, and celebrate milestones and victories along the way.

RESOURCES

Recommended Reading List for Further Growth:

1. "RICH Relationships Refuge Our Marital Code to Oneness' Workbook Gil & Renée M Beavers

2. "The Meaning of Marriage: Facing the Complexities of Commitment with the Wisdom of God" by Timothy Keller

3. "Sacred Marriage: What If God Designed Marriage to Make Us Holy More Than to Make Us Happy?" by Gary L. Thomas

4. "The Five Love Languages: The Secret to Love That Lasts" by Gary Chapman

5. "Boundaries in Dating: How Healthy Choices Grow Healthy Relationships" by Henry Cloud and John Townsend

6. "Love & Respect: The Love She Most Desires; The Respect He Desperately Needs" by Emerson Eggerichs

7. "The Mingling of Souls: God's Design for Love, Marriage, Sex, and Redemption" by Matt Chandler

8. "Emotionally Healthy Relationships: Discipleship that Deeply Changes Your Relationship with Others" by Peter Scazzero

9. "You and Me Forever: Marriage in Light of Eternity" by Francis Chan and Lisa Chan

10. "Sheet Music: Uncovering the Secrets of Sexual Intimacy in Marriage" by Kevin Leman

11. "The Seven Principles for Making Marriage Work: A Practical Guide from the Country's Foremost Relationship Expert" by John Gottman and Nan Silver

Resources for Seeking Counseling and Support:

1. RICH Relationships Refuge (https//www.richrrmarriagementors.com/)
2. National Marriage Encounter (https://wwme.org/)
3. Focus on the Family Marriage Counseling (https://www.focusonthefamily.com/marriage/marriagegettinghelpforyourrelationship/)
4. American Association for Marriage and Family Therapy (https://www.aamft.org/)
5. Prepare/Enrich (https://www.prepareenrich.com/)

6. Community Bible Church (https://www.communitybible.com /merge)
7. Samaritan Counseling Centers (https://samaritancc.org/)
8. Online Therapy Platforms (e.g., Better Help, talk space) These platforms offer convenient and accessible counseling services for individuals and couples.

Milton Keynes UK
Ingram Content Group UK Ltd.
UKHW052245280524
443311UK00008B/150

9 798218 425210